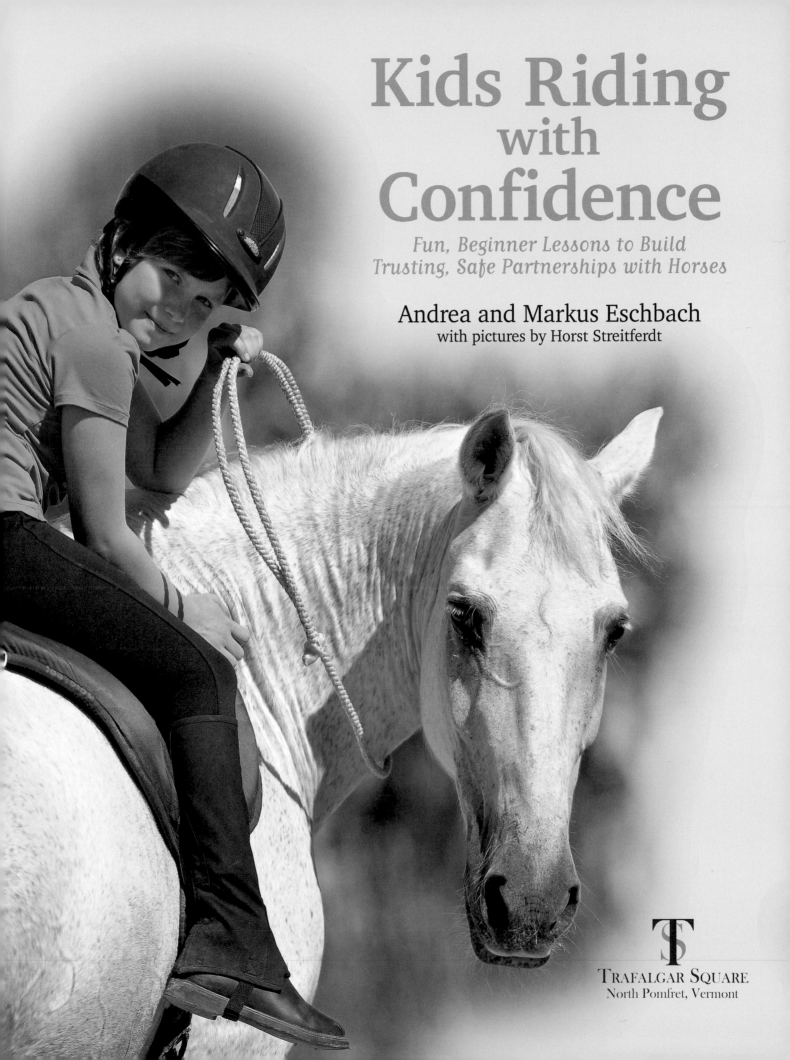

Kids Riding with Confidence

Fun, Beginner Lessons to Build
Trusting, Safe Partnerships with Horses

Andrea and Markus Eschbach
with pictures by Horst Streitferdt

T S

TRAFALGAR SQUARE
North Pomfret, Vermont

First published in 2014 by
Trafalgar Square Books
North Pomfret, Vermont 05053

Originally published in the German language as *Reiten mit Vertrauen* by Franckh-Kosmos
Verlags-GmbH & Co. KG, Stuttgart

Disclaimer of Liability
The authors and publisher shall have neither liability nor responsibility to any person or entity with
respect to any loss or damage caused or alleged to be caused directly or indirectly by the information
contained in this book. While the book is as accurate as the authors can make it, there may be
errors, omissions, and inaccuracies.

**Trafalgar Square Books encourages the use of approved safety helmets in all equestrian sports
and activities.**

ISBN: 978-1-57076-706-7

Library of Congress Control Number: 2014944446

All photos by Horst Streitferdt, Stuttgart, *except:* p. 1, Christiane Slawik, Würzburg; p. 21,
p. 22, p. 23, by Andrea and Markus Eschbach, Waldshut-Tiengen.

Cover design by RM Didier
Translation by Emma Josephine Didier
Typefaces: Charter ITC by BT, Matrix Script

Printed in the United States of America

10 9 8 7 6 5 4 3 2 1

Contents

Hello!

Do you spend every minute you can at the nearest stable? Are horses your favorite animals? Maybe your parents have finally said you can have riding lessons, and now all you can think about is sitting on the broad back of a horse, feeling the wind against your face, riding through the woods and fields with your friends...

We want to show you how to take care of your horse before you ride, while you ride, and after you ride. We train horses to be ridden with what's known as a "bitless bridle," which helps control the direction of the horse without using a bit; this works well for our horses and our students because we have taught our horses on the ground to have great trust in people. A bitless bridle means an accidental tug on the reins won't hurt or scare the horse.

In this book, we will show you how to groom and tack up correctly; get started in the saddle; sit on, steer, and stop the horse; ride through obstacles and prepare for the trail; and even ride bareback, with no bridle at all! In the end, you'll have a trusting friend and partner in your horse.

We hope you have fun!

Andrea
and
Markus

Horse Language

An important part of riding is to **get to know** your horse and **earn his trust.** It helps to know a few words in **"horse language"** so that you and your horse can understand each other. Do you know how horses say "Hello"? The photos on these two pages are a "mini dictionary" of some of the things horses say. (We cover this topic in more detail in our book *How to Speak Horse*.)

"Hello, who are you?"

When your horse trusts you, he lets you be close to him.

"I like you, and you like me!"

"Please keep scratching my itchy spot!"

Horses are naturally skittish and careful, and they usually don't trust us immediately. That's because, as grass-eating animals in the wild, they were prey. This means they were hunted and eaten if they weren't paying attention! Therefore, horses see everything they're unfamiliar with as a threat—including us. Horses must learn that we're harmless and they can trust us. Unfortunately, we often move quickly, make loud noises, handle them too roughly, or hold them in one spot so they can't run away. All of these behaviors are also typical of predators.

Look at your own face in the mirror: In a lot of ways, it looks like the face of a big cat or predator, doesn't it?

"I'm resting."

"I don't like you; go away! I'm warning you!"

Your eyes are next to each other at the front of your head, like those of a predator.

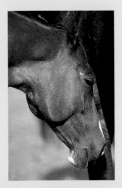

"If you get any closer, I'll bite you."

"I'm tired."

"What's going on over there?"

When we know a little "horse language," it's easier for us to explain to horses that we mean them no harm. Clear communication lets us slowly build a friendship. When a horse becomes your friend, he'll be much more willing to let you touch him, put a halter on him, or sit on his back.

"I feel comfortable and safe with my friends."

The First Step to Becoming Friends

Before you can ride your horse, you have to prepare him: Putting on his halter, cleaning his hooves, and currying and brushing him are all an important part of riding.

Body brushes

Curry combs

Tail brush

Hoof pick

It helps to lay out all the tools you'll need before you start grooming your horse.

ANDREA'S TIP

Grooming the horse is very important because it removes sand and dirt from his coat—if too much gets stuck under the saddle, it could irritate his skin. Standing still for haltering and grooming is one of the first things a young horse needs to learn, and simple everyday chores like this will help you get to know your horse better. Building a friendship begins with grooming!

The *halter* is used to lead a horse from the ground. Hold the halter open invitingly, lift it so that the nose piece is in place, and gently pull the head piece over the ears.

If the horse is willing to lower his head to help you put the halter on, that's a good sign that he's started to trust you.

When you tie your horse to a fence or post, use a quick-release knot, which can easily be undone in an emergency. Always make sure you tie your horse to a stable post or a ring securely fastened to a wall. A wobbly fence or cracked board could splinter or break if your horse pulls back against it, and your horse could panic and hurt himself or you. Tie the knot so it's at about the height of the horse's nose, and leave enough slack to give him a comfortable amount of standing room—but never so much that the rope hangs down far enough for him to step on it or get tangled in it.

To tie a quick-release knot, wrap the lead rope around a sturdy rail or stable post ①. Make a loop with the loose end and hold it over the first part of the rope ②. Reach through the loop and past the first part of the rope, and grab the loose end of the rope, pulling it through the first loop to form a new loop. Reach through the new loop and repeat ③. A sharp tug on the remaining tail of the knot should undo it. Practice doing and undoing this knot before using it to tie your horse.

Once your horse is safely tied, curry and brush his body, paying careful attention to his itchy spots, sore spots, and favorite places to get rubbed.

MARKUS'S TIP

It's always safest to stand next to the horse's shoulder.

Brush the horse's **mane and tail** carefully, strand by strand.

Clean the horse's **hooves**: gently remove rocks, soil, and mud with the hoof pick.

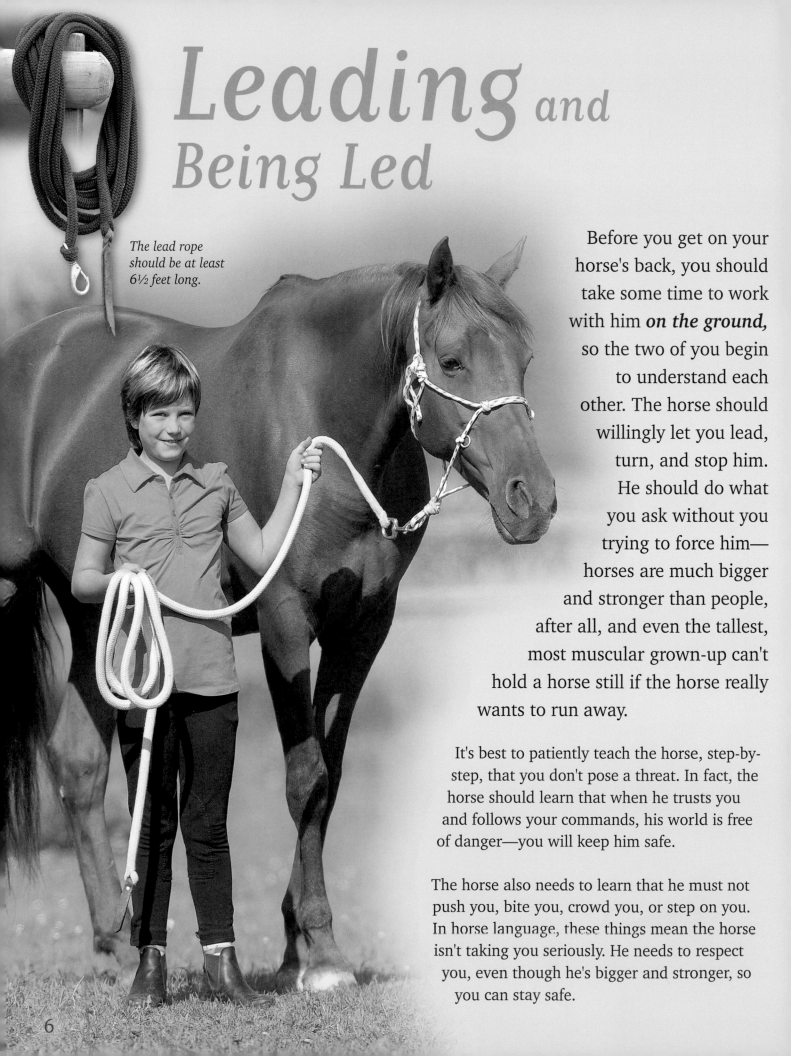

Leading and Being Led

The lead rope should be at least 6½ feet long.

Before you get on your horse's back, you should take some time to work with him **on the ground,** so the two of you begin to understand each other. The horse should willingly let you lead, turn, and stop him. He should do what you ask without you trying to force him—horses are much bigger and stronger than people, after all, and even the tallest, most muscular grown-up can't hold a horse still if the horse really wants to run away.

It's best to patiently teach the horse, step-by-step, that you don't pose a threat. In fact, the horse should learn that when he trusts you and follows your commands, his world is free of danger—you will keep him safe.

The horse also needs to learn that he must not push you, bite you, crowd you, or step on you. In horse language, these things mean the horse isn't taking you seriously. He needs to respect you, even though he's bigger and stronger, so you can stay safe.

Lead your horse with a nylon, leather, or rope halter and a long cotton rope. Most lead ropes are too short. A rope that's at least 6½ feet long is best, because you'll have plenty of room to stay safe even if your horse jumps, shies, or startles while you're walking.

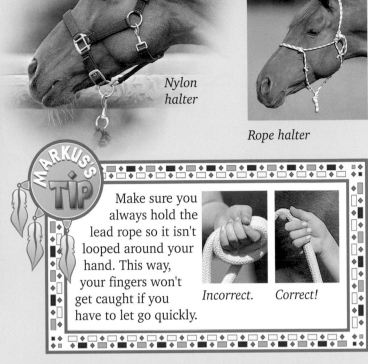

Nylon halter

Rope halter

You can lead your horse from either side. Walk at his shoulder, and watch his head and ears: They will tell you what he's thinking and whether he's paying attention to you.

MARKUS'S TIP

Make sure you always hold the lead rope so it isn't looped around your hand. This way, your fingers won't get caught if you have to let go quickly.

Incorrect. *Correct!*

Practice leading your horse from the front—get an adult to help your horse learn to follow you, the first few times you try this. Learn to "hear" where your horse is, even when he's behind you.

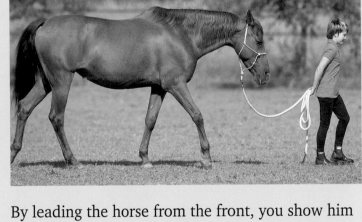

By leading the horse from the front, you show him that you know where to go, you know what's ahead, and it's okay to follow your lead. If he trusts you and feels safe with you, he'll come readily.

A round pen or small fenced-in area is a great place to play "Follow the Leader." Once you've made friends with your horse, you can ask him to walk, turn, and stop with you, without using a halter or lead rope at all—just your body movement. The horse will decide whether to follow you or move away; his reactions will tell you whether he understands what you want, and whether he really trusts you.

What You Need

When working around or riding your horse, **sturdy, closed-toed shoes** are a must. Non-slip soles and small heels will keep your feet from getting stuck in the stirrups. Comfortable *riding pants* are another great addition to your birthday wish list! Above all, you'll want to wear clothes that let you move freely—and that are okay to get dirty.

Helmet

A good riding helmet will protect you from serious head injury if you fall.

Saddle Types

The **bareback pad** ④ *is secured to the horse's back with a girth. It protects the horse's back and cushions the rider's seat—it's a nice way to ride (almost) bareback. The lack of stirrups teaches you to balance and maintain a relaxed sitting position on the horse.*

A **Western saddle** ① *is comfortable for casual rides and trail rides, and provides good support for the rider.*

For longer riding excursions, adding a **sheepskin seat cover** *over a Western saddle* ② *may be a good idea.*

The classic **all-purpose English saddle** ③ *works for beginning flatwork, dressage, jumping, and trail riding.*

Saddling Up

Most saddles weigh between 11 and 15 pounds and some are even heavier, so it might be a good idea to get some help saddling up. Your instructor should explain how to put the saddle on properly, and should check to make sure you've done it correctly.

The saddle must fit the horse, and it must be put on correctly. If it doesn't fit well or isn't in the right spot, it can be uncomfortable—even painful—for the horse.

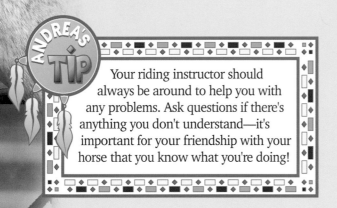

ANDREA'S TIP

Your riding instructor should always be around to help you with any problems. Ask questions if there's anything you don't understand—it's important for your friendship with your horse that you know what you're doing!

This saddle fits well and is correctly placed.

Bridle

We teach our students to ride without a metal bit in the horse's mouth. Riding a horse with a bitless bridle is easy. You can control, direct, and stop your horse just as well without using a bit, and the horse's sensitive mouth isn't hurt accidentally as you learn to control your body and hands while in the saddle.

Here is one example of a bitless bridle. There are many different kinds available.

Put the bridle reins over the horse's head so they're looped over his neck. Then, holding the bridle in your left hand, take off the horse's halter.

First, the bridle goes over the nose; then gently pull the head piece over the ears.

Finally, buckle the noseband and throatlatch. Leave enough slack for one or two fingers to fit between the straps and the horse's head.

Get in the Saddle!

Now it's time to get on your horse! The horse's back is pretty high up, isn't it? You might be wondering how you're supposed to get up there without a ladder! Don't worry, there are lots of tricks to help you mount up—even if you're short!

Before getting on, always check the girth's tightness so you know the saddle won't suddenly slip to one side. You can adjust it once you're in the saddle, too.

MARKUS'S TIP

If your horse suddenly seems enormous and your heart starts to pound, that's all right! It's normal to be afraid sometimes: Being scared can save us from dangerous situations, and that's a good thing! Turn to your teacher or the adult with you if you're frightened—he or she can help you feel a little braver.

Practice *mounting and dismounting* a few times in a row—this will help make the movements onto and off of the horse feel more natural.

Stand facing the horse. Adjust the stirrup so your left foot can reach it, and use it as a step.

Move as close to the horse as you can. Hold on to the horse's neck or the saddle, and push off the ground with your right foot.

Swing your right leg over the horse, being careful not to kick him, and settle into the saddle. Your instructor can help hold the saddle still, if necessary.

Now try dismounting. The basic dismount is easy: Take your feet out of the stirrups, swing your right leg back over the horse, and lower yourself down. But there's also another way to do it.

*Take your feet out of the stirrups, and then move your right leg **forward** over the saddle.*

You'll be sitting sideways on the horse...

...and you can jump down easily. Make sure you land on both feet, and look before you leap!

If you're still afraid of falling, you can play a little game to help you practice until you feel more confident.

Ask your horse to walk beside you along the rail in the riding arena. While he's walking, mount! Then, after letting him keep walking a little way with you in the saddle, dismount— while he's still walking. This will help you learn to mount and dismount quickly and easily, even when the horse is moving.

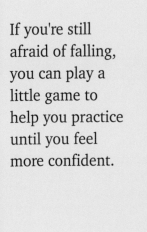

Off You Go!

You made it! Now that you're up on your horse, it's all about making sure you can communicate clearly with him from "up there."

Correct: Maureen is sitting up straight and she's relaxed and balanced.

Incorrect: You don't want to lean too far forward or too far back!

The Rider's Seat

The most important thing is to make sure you're seated well. You will learn the "rider's seat," which will help you stay balanced and comfortable even with all the shakes, sways, and bumps from being on a moving horse.

The Feet

You can "park" your feet in the stirrups. This means you place one foot in each stirrup, and apply just enough pressure to make sure they don't slip out. The "floor" of the stirrup should rest against the ball of your foot; if it's against your toes, you may lose it, and if it's against your heel, you may get stuck!

Rest your foot on the stirrup with your ankle relaxed and your sole flat, as if you're standing on the ground.

If you pull your heel up, you could lose your balance, or your ability to give commands ("aids") with your legs.

The Hands

Hold the reins with both hands and close your fists loosely. Keep your wrists straight. Hold the reins in the air, just above the horse's mane.

Correct!

Incorrect.

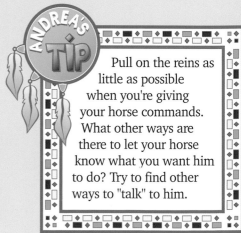

ANDREA'S TIP

Pull on the reins as little as possible when you're giving your horse commands. What other ways are there to let your horse know what you want him to do? Try to find other ways to "talk" to him.

A Mini Stretching Lesson

Since your horse is going to need to move around with you on his back, you have to learn how to move along with him. If you're too stiff, you'll just rattle around in the saddle, which won't be comfortable for either of you. To help you stay loose when the horse starts moving, try this mini stretching lesson as a warm-up.

As an exercise, try guiding your horse while holding the reins in only one hand. This will teach you to steer using your seat, legs, and eyes (looking in the direction you want to go) instead of just the reins.

Make yourself tall by stretching your arms and fingers toward the sky.

Reach across and down with your opposite hand and try to touch your toes.

Turn in the saddle until you can see your horse's tail, and then repeat on the other side. Maureen turns far enough to get a high five!

You can try all kinds of little stretches while your horse is standing or walking. They'll make you loose and flexible, and teach you to stay balanced—and they're fun! It's also good to practice letting go of the reins sometimes. You shouldn't need to hold on to them to stay in the saddle.

Lean forward and give your horse a hug! Pet his mane from his withers to his crest—how far can you reach?

13

How the Rider's Aids "Talk" to the Horse

Once you're ready to ride, you need to tell your horse where to go, when, and how fast. For every command, imagine exactly what you want your horse to do, as if you're *painting a picture in your head*. The more detailed you can make your picture, the clearer your commands will be, and the better your body will know what it's supposed to do.

Walk On

Once you have a mental image of you and your horse moving together at a walk, breathe in, and touch both of your lower legs to the horse's sides at the same time, at the girth. Clicking your tongue can also tell your horse that he should "walk on." Try to make a habit of looking and turning your shoulders in the direction you want to ride. That way, your body automatically indicates to the horse where he's supposed to go.

MARKUS'S TIP

When your horse has done what you wanted, relax your feet and legs so you aren't putting pressure on the horse's sides anymore. Taking away the pressure like this lets the horse know that he did the right thing, and he'll react even more quickly the next time. Only press with your legs again if you want the horse to speed up.

Turning

Of course, you won't want to just ride your horse in a straight line. Whenever you want to turn, picture riding in a wide arc, and set your eyes on the spot you want to reach. Let's say you want to turn left: Look to the left and press your right leg against the horse's side just behind the girth. Your left leg should also put pressure on the horse's side, but should remain at the girth, like it did when you wanted to go forward. Once you've signaled with your body and legs, you can also use the reins by pulling the left rein slightly toward your stomach—just enough to move the horse's nose in the direction you want to turn. The horse will follow his nose.

You only need to pull on the reins enough to move the horse's nose.

When your horse responds to your command to turn, relax your legs and ease off on the rein so you aren't putting pressure on the horse anymore. You should only keep the pressure on if your horse still needs help understanding what you want him to do.

Sink into the saddle with your weight in your heels.

Slowing and Halting

The most important aids you need to know are those that tell your horse to slow down and stop. Your horse should be trained to halt right away, on cue, in any situation—whether you're leading him from the ground, practicing in the arena, or riding out on the trail. It's the only way to make sure you're always safe!

Here's how to slow to a halt: As you walk along, imagine your horse slowing down, lowering his head, and coming to a relaxed stop. Breathe out and sink into the saddle—you should feel like you're making yourself "heavier" in your seat, as though there are small weights attached to your heels. Help your horse understand what you want with a quiet, drawn-out "Whooooooa." If your horse still hasn't come to a stop, take on the reins a little bit—shorten them by drawing them in slightly toward your belly button. Never jerk on the reins to cue your horse to stop; this could hurt or spook him! Once your horse has stopped, relax your body and release the tension on the reins.

If the horse hasn't stopped, take on the reins a bit.

Once the horse stops, relax and let off the pressure.

15

Pick Up the *Pace!*

Once you're confident and stable in the saddle at a walk, it's time to step it up a notch! Remember, even when your horse is moving at a faster gait, you should still be able to keep a relaxed and flexible seat.

Trot/Jog

This is your horse's second "gear," and it is a bit faster than the walk. To ask your horse to move up to a trot from a walk, paint a picture of trotting in your mind. Breathe in, lightly press your legs against your horse's

sides, and click your tongue to ask him to move forward more quickly.

When the horse trots nice and slow, it's easy to stay seated in the saddle and let your body follow the movements of the horse. This is called "sitting trot." When the horse trots faster, it's best to "post," or do the "rising trot," because it's more comfortable for both of you when the horse is moving a lot. Just lift yourself a little way out of the saddle and then sit again—make the "one-two" of the horse's stride into "lift-sit." You'll both be happier!

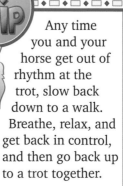

ANDREA'S TIP

Any time you and your horse get out of rhythm at the trot, slow back down to a walk. Breathe, relax, and get back in control, and then go back up to a trot together.

Canter/Lope

This gait is even faster than the trot. It feels different from the walk or the trot, more of a swinging or rocking motion. We bet you already know the first aid you'll need: That's right, your mental picture! Once you are ready, take a deep breath and look ahead down the side of the arena. If you're cantering to the left (around a left-hand curve, for instance), press your left leg against the horse at the girth and swing your right leg back, "pushing" the horse into the canter with your seat. It should feel almost like trying to go higher on a playground swing—but make sure you're sitting up straight, and do the "pushing" with just your hips. You don't want to lose your balance in the saddle.

The canter feels a bit faster than the other gaits! In a Western saddle, you can hold on to the horn the first few times you try cantering; you can also hold the pommel of an English saddle, if necessary.

Backing Up:
The "Closed Door" Drill

To ask your horse to back up, paint your mental picture: Imagine your horse walking backward step by step. Then lift the reins so you have a steady contact with the horse—without pulling back on them. Just hold them with even tension.

Now use your seat: Stick out your bottom like a duck and press both legs lightly against your horse's sides. The horse may want to walk forward because your legs are telling him to, but you've "closed the door" in front with the tension on the reins. The doors to the left and right—the options to turn—are also closed by your legs. Only the back door is open: By sticking out your bottom, you've shifted your weight forward slightly, and left your horse's back end free. As soon as your horse takes even one tentative step backward, release your aids (relax your legs, sit back, and ease the tension on the reins) right away and praise him.

To back up, put steady pressure on the reins, and stick out your bottom like a duck.

Release your aids and praise your horse the moment he takes a step backward.

The Riding Playground

To make sure you and your horse don't get bored, make your arena a fun place to be: Create a ***riding playground*** where you and your horse can learn and practice all kinds of useful skills. For example, it's important that your horse not get scared and spook when you're riding out on the trail and a branch breaks loudly, or if you need to ride past someone who has a dog or is holding an umbrella. You can help your horse learn to be brave by turning scenarios like these into games—but if your horse hasn't done anything like this before, you should start by leading him through the playground by hand. Ask your riding instructor to make sure your games are safe.

First, you want to get your horse used to encountering new situations and objects. Most horses have trouble with this—it's a horse's nature to be careful when stepping on uneven ground or passing by objects that move or flutter.

It can be a lot of fun to help your horse get used to strange objects!

Fast-moving objects—like a colorful ball—can make horses nervous. If you practice riding near them with your horse, you can help him learn to "stay cool."

Can you help your horse stay calm near someone who's opening an umbrella?

Create a "pool" of balloons, and ask your horse to trust you enough to walk through it. The added challenge is the noise it'll make if he pops one! This game is best when you're secure in the saddle, in case your horse startles.

Set up a narrow aisle for your horse to walk through using tarps draped over jumps.

Practice with streamers in the ring to make it easier to ride past low branches on the trail.

19

The *Obstacle* Course

After practicing in your playground, try turning some of the games into an **obstacle course**. This will help you when you're out riding on the trail, since you might face several tough spots in a row.

From up here, the world looks even more beautiful: Benji loves stepping up onto this platform!

The best thing about riding through your own obstacle course is that you can practice as many times as you want, so even if you aren't very experienced or your horse has trouble with some obstacles, you can keep trying until you get good at it. You should get to know your horse first, though, and an adult or your instructor should be with you.

Weaving through cones can be tough when you have big feet...

...but with practice, it's easy!

Give your horse a horse-sized "soccer" ball— can he roll it into a goal?

For an extra challenge, try riding part of the course with only a halter and a lead rope.

Pool noodles and mats teach your horse to lift his feet over debris or fallen logs.

Benji stays on track even with only one rein!

ANDREA'S TIP

Have you noticed that you put in more effort when there's a specific riding "task" you want to master? When you ride in the ring with markers or obstacles, your eyes have an "anchor," so you can plan where you want to ride and how you're going to get there. You might even "paint that picture" in your mind! Your horse can tell when this is happening; it makes your aids easy to follow.

21

Let's Go Outside!

Now you're ready to start thinking about the real-life obstacles that the **outside world** has for you when you're on horseback.

Outside the arena, you have to watch out for all kinds of new things that might be difficult or scary for your horse. This manhole cover could be slippery if your horse has metal shoes on.

Always look ahead when riding on the trail so you can approach and clear obstacles like this log easily and safely.

When you're riding uphill, you can help your horse out by leaning forward in the saddle. Be careful, though—you need to do this without pulling on the reins.

Training Your Reflexes

When people get scared or nervous, we automatically try to curl up into a ball. This happens so fast we don't even think about it—our bodies react on their own to protect us. This is called a *reflex*. It's supposed to be helpful, but it's not a good idea when you're riding! If you react this way, your upper body will go forward and you'll pull your arms and legs in toward you—in the saddle, you'll lose your balance, and then you'll probably try to fix it by gripping with your legs (which tells your horse to go faster) and pulling on the reins (which can hurt your horse's mouth, if you're riding with a bit). This won't help your horse calm down, and can turn a scary situation into a dangerous one.

It helps to practice reacting a new way: When you feel scared or nervous, lean back, hold your legs away from the horse, and keep your arms out and forward (see photo below). This keeps you balanced without scaring your horse!

When you're riding downhill, lean back a little bit, and try not to get in your horse's way while he finds the best places to step.

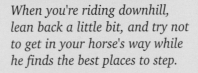

MARKUS'S TIP

- Prepare for the kinds of things you might run into out on the trail with your playground and your obstacle course exercises.
- Practice mounting and dismounting on both sides of your horse—you never know where or when you might have to get on or off!
- Outside the arena, there's all kinds of things that can distract you or your horse: passing cars, tractors in fields, birds in the bushes, fluttering banners, or barking dogs. You'll have to pay extra close attention to everything around you so things like these don't catch you by surprise!
- When riding with an adult or your instructor, always listen to what he or she says and always stay behind him or her.
- After riding on the trail, check your horse really carefully for sore or chafed spots or scratches, and be especially thorough when you clean your horse's hooves.

When you ride out on the trail, you have to be attentive and keep looking ahead so you're prepared for any obstacles in the way and won't be startled by birds flying out of the brush or sudden noises. If you're calm and focused, your horse will feel safe, and he'll enjoy riding outside the arena just as much as you do!

Riding Free:
Bareback and Bridleless

Do you wonder what it's like to sit on nothing but a bareback pad or ride bareback entirely? What about using a loop of rope instead of a bridle and two reins?

The smooth coat and rounded back of a horse aren't the same as a saddle—riding bareback is a skill that needs to be learned. The ideal horse for this is calm and dependable, because you'll slide around a bit as you learn how to stay on the horse's back while he's moving. You'll get rocked forward and backward, left and right; in order to stay balanced, you'll need to follow the horse's movements. Don't just sit there and hope you won't fall! Move as if you're trying to "help" your horse trot or walk forward. If you don't move with him, or you sit too stiffly, you'll start to slip.

Riding bareback with a neck rope is a challenge at first—but it's also a pretty great feeling!

Make sure you're sitting right behind your horse's withers—this is the most comfortable for both of you.

Riding bareback will quickly teach you how to keep your balance, and it will help you develop a better seat. You'll be able to feel your horse's muscles moving underneath you, and you'll find that your horse is quicker to do what you ask—he can feel *you* better without the saddle, too! After riding bareback a few times, ride with the saddle again, and notice how you're practically "glued" to it.

The neck rope should hang loosely around the horse's neck. You can buy these premade from waxed lasso rope, and they are usually adjustable.

Less is More

Can you still guide and steer your horse well when all you have is a neck rope?

This is a good test of your riding aids. You can hold the neck rope with one or both hands. Only use it when you need it to tell your horse what to do. Hold it so it hangs loosely and doesn't bother your horse.

Remember, the most important aids aren't given with the reins, but with where you look, your seat, and your legs. Using the neck rope lets you practice using those aids more.

If you don't have a neck rope, you can tie a lead rope loosely around your horse's neck and use that.

When you do it right, it's almost like dancing!

And Don't Forget...

Riding, playing with, and just being around your horse is supposed to be fun! And taking good care of your horse is part of the fun. This includes everything you do after riding, like unsaddling, brushing your horse again, and if your horse has been sweating, cleaning any sticky spots with a sponge. When it's hot, you can also bathe your horse with a sponge and some water, or spray him with a hose.

MARKUS'S TIP

When you're brushing or massaging your horse after a ride, pay close attention to spots that make your horse twitch, or where his coat is rough or seems chafed. Check for scratches and thorns, and inspect his hooves for stones or debris. Remember, you can always ask your riding instructor for help or advice!

Having the girth loosened after you dismount is very relaxing for your horse. Afterward, lead him around the ring a few times—the movement of the saddle as he walks will give him a gentle back massage.

If your horse isn't too hot after your ride, offer him some water. If he's very sweaty, wait until he's cooled off a bit before giving him a drink.

After unsaddling, massage your horse's back by gently running your palm down along his spine.

Always tell your horse that you had a great ride together, that you love being with him, and that he did well. Thank him for carrying you on his back. He might not understand the words, but he'll still know what you're saying if you say it from the heart.

Something We
Care About

There are many kids like you out there: All they want to do is ride horses. It's very important to us to make it clear that riding is more than just sitting on a horse; and a horse is not just a piece of sports equipment, but a living being with a body, mind, and soul, and emotions just like yours. We want you to learn more than just the beginnings of good riding technique—empathy and understanding for the horse can be learned, too. Developing this kind of awareness of and respect for your horse will give you a solid foundation on which to build a life with horses.

We thank everyone who helped us make this book!

Other great horse books for kids:

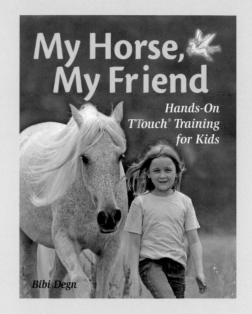

Andrea & Markus Eschbach, authors of *Riding Free*

How to Speak Horse

Simple Groundwork Lessons

A Horse-Crazy Kid's Guide to
Reading Body Language and "Talking Back"

My Horse, My Friend

Hands-On
TTouch® Training
for Kids

Bibi Degn

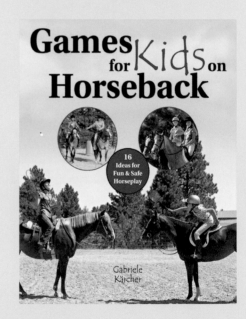

Games for Kids on Horseback

16 Ideas for
Fun & Safe
Horseplay

Gabriele Kärcher